YOUNG GEOGRAPHER

NATURAL RESOURCES

DAMIAN RANDLE

Thomson Learning • New York

Young Geographer

The Changing Earth
Food and Farming
Journeys
Natural Resources
Protecting the Planet
Settlements
Transportation
Use of Land
The World's Population
The World's Weather

Front cover: A hydroelectric power plant in the Andes.
Back cover: A forester chopping wood.
Frontispiece: Coal miners working underground.

First published in the
United States in 1993 by
Thomson Learning
115 Fifth Avenue
New York, NY 10003

First published in 1992 by
Wayland (Publishers) Ltd.

Copyright © 1992 Wayland (Publishers) Ltd.

U.S. version copyright © 1993 Thomson Learning

Cataloging-in-Publication Data applied for

ISBN: 1-56847-056-8

Printed in Italy

Contents

Introduction	4
Extracting resources	6
Processing raw materials	10
Energy resources	14
Creating power	18
The environment	22
Water	26
Recycling	28
Glossary	30
Books to read	31
Notes for activities	31
Index	32

All the words that are in **bold** appear in the glossary on page 30.

Introduction

All over the world, people use natural **resources** to fill their basic survival needs. Natural resources are materials that come from the earth. They are found on the land, in the sea, and under the ground. Some of these resources can be used as they are found, but others have to be converted into different forms before they can be used.

Our basic needs for survival include shelter, a supply of energy, water, and tools. For shelter, people often build houses out of materials from the ground, such as stone and brick, or out of wood. Wood is also burned to provide energy, although today most energy is produced by burning **fossil fuels**, which are taken from the ground.

Water from a well at Matmata in Tunisia. Simple wells are the only water supply in many parts of the world.

Wood is the main material used for the framework of this house.

Although people can sometimes survive without shelter or fuel, no one can survive without water. Water is our most important resource. Despite this, about two billion people in the world do not have a reliable supply of clean water.

Tools are not as precious as water, but life would be difficult without them. In the modern industrial world, tools are often large and complex machines. These machines are used for **manufacturing** goods. To make these machines we need metal. All metals come from **ores**, which are found in rock.

As the world's population grows, more resources are needed. However, we cannot just go on digging out and chopping down Earth's resources. Some are running low, and, once used up, they cannot be replaced. Our use of resources can also cause **pollution**. We need to be careful about the environmental effects of using resources. We should use less and recycle more.

Extracting resources

Metals and other **minerals** are removed from the earth, or mined, in two main ways. People usually think of mines as underground pits, but strip mines are about three times more common. This type of mining is possible when the metal ores lie near the surface. The entire soil layer is removed from an area of land. Then the metals are taken out by huge **walking draglines** and **bucket-wheel excavators**.

A dragline digging coal in Australia. This method can remove large amounts of coal, but can also damage the landscape.

A miner working in an underground tunnel of a gold mine.

To mine underground, shafts from the surface are dug deep into the ground – sometimes to depths of over 10,000 feet. Tunnels lead off the main shaft. In an underground mine, the material has to be moved from the tunnels to the shaft, often a distance of several miles, and then hoisted to the surface. The mines require a **ventilation** system to provide air and a cooling system deep underground where it is very hot.

The seas are used to provide many important resources and are likely to be used even more in the future. Sea water contains many valuable **elements** including uranium, gold, and silver, but the only ones that can be extracted cheaply at the moment are magnesium, bromine, and potassium.

Some resources can be extracted from the seabed. Important ones today include tin, gold, and phosphates. In the next century much of the world's mining may be on, or just under, the seabed. Currently a great deal of work is being done to develop ways of scraping manganese deposits off deep seabeds.

These softwood trees have been cut from conifer plantations.

Wood is believed to be the third most valuable item in the world trade, after oil and gas. Trees are cut down in ancient natural forests around the world. But this cannot go on forever. Wood is a **renewable** resource – but people must make the effort to grow at least as many trees as they cut down.

Forestry is now a highly **mechanized** industry, and a great deal of wood comes from plantations that are "farmed." This involves mechanized planting, transplanting, thinning, and cropping. The forester drains, **fertilizes**, and prepares the land in ways similar to those of the farmer. In temperate climates the main timber crop is the conifer, a fast-growing softwood that has many uses, particularly for furniture-making and construction.

Rain forests are mainly located in the tropics – the hot, humid areas near the equator. The trees there are hardwoods, which grow more slowly than softwoods and are very valuable. The tropical rain forests may disappear because they are being cut down and not replaced. To help save the rain forests, forest plantations are now being started by organizations throughout the world.

The Green Belt Movement, Kenya

In Kenya, the Green Belt Movement organizes the growing of hundreds of seedlings in small tree nurseries throughout the country. The trees provide much-needed firewood for villagers and also keep the soil from being **eroded** from food-growing plots.

The Movement was started in 1975 by Professor Wangari Maathai, who encouraged local people to take part. Women are paid a small amount for each tree that survives. School children help with the planting. Most of the trees are successful because the people in the Movement take good care of them.

In just one year the Movement planted more trees than the government planted in ten years. By 1992, there were more than 600 tree nurseries, and, with the help of 50,000 women and 3,000 schools, they had planted more than 12 million trees.

These trees are growing in a softwood plantation in Kenya.

Processing raw materials

Smelting is used to produce metals like iron, lead, copper, and zinc from ores. An ore is heated to a very high temperature in a **blast furnace**. The hot air that is blasted in makes the fuel and the ore burn more fiercely. The **molten** metal flows out of the furnace and can then be shaped or treated again.

Iron is usually treated again to form steel. Cast iron is produced by the blast furnace, but iron has **impurities** in it and is not strong enough or rustproof enough to have many uses. Instead it is made into steel. Very high temperatures are needed to convert the iron into steel. Carbon is added for strength.

A worker pouring hot, molten steel. In liquid form, steel is easy to cast.

Other metals can also be added to give the steel particular qualities. Chromium and nickel are added to make stainless steel, for example.

The other way to convert ore into metal is the electrical **refining** method. By passing an electrical current through certain mixtures the different materials in the mixture can be separated. Aluminum ore or bauxite may be mixed with another mineral, cryolite. When the strong electric current is passed through, the aluminum splits off as a liquid. It can then be made into anything from pots and pans to aircraft parts.

Checking the thin strip of aluminum as it comes out from the rollers.

A long ribbon of flat glass moves on rollers to be washed and cut.

Pottery and glass, two of the most useful materials, are called **ceramics**. Like metals, they are made from resources found in the ground. Clay is first shaped, sometimes by hand and sometimes by machine. It is then baked in an oven at a very high temperature to make pottery. Clay can be shaped to make anything from drinking cups to bricks.

To make glass, **silica sand** is mixed with other materials like soda ash and limestone, then melted at about 2,700°F. The mixture can be "floated" out over a smooth surface to form flat sheets for windows, or molded and blown into bottles. Different types of glass can be made by adding ingredients such as lead or borax.

Right These vast quantities of wood chips will be used to make pulp for paper.

Sheets of pulp are mixed with water to make the liquid used in papermaking.

Wood has been used since prehistoric times in almost every part of the world. It has many uses and is fairly cheap to buy and convert. Converting used to mean just chopping down trees and cutting up the wood to make furniture, frames for building houses, or tools. But today the wood from many softwood trees is turned into tiny chips that are mixed with chemicals to make wood **pulp** for paper. They can also be used to make particleboard.

Converting raw materials into useful products can damage the environment because of waste and pollution. Today industries have to be more **efficient** by recovering waste and, where possible, cutting down on air and water pollution.

Energy resources

In addition to wood, there are three types of resources used to produce energy. The first is fossil fuels, which are extracted from the earth. The second is a mineral – uranium, which is used for nuclear power. The third type is alternative energy, such as solar, wind, or water power.

Coal is a fossil fuel extracted from the earth by strip and deep-pit mining. Oil and gas are extracted from the ground by drilling. The biggest reserves of oil in the world are in the Middle East, around the Persian Gulf.

The biggest gas producers are the United States and Russia. In Europe the main area for drilling gas is the North Sea. The area is shared by several countries. Australia has coal and some oil and gas.

Oil and gas, which are often found together, are so valuable that it is worth spending large sums of money to find them. Satellite photographs are studied to find the type of rock formations that indicate the presence of these fuels. Aircraft use equipment like **radar** and **magnetic sensors** to find places that seem promising.

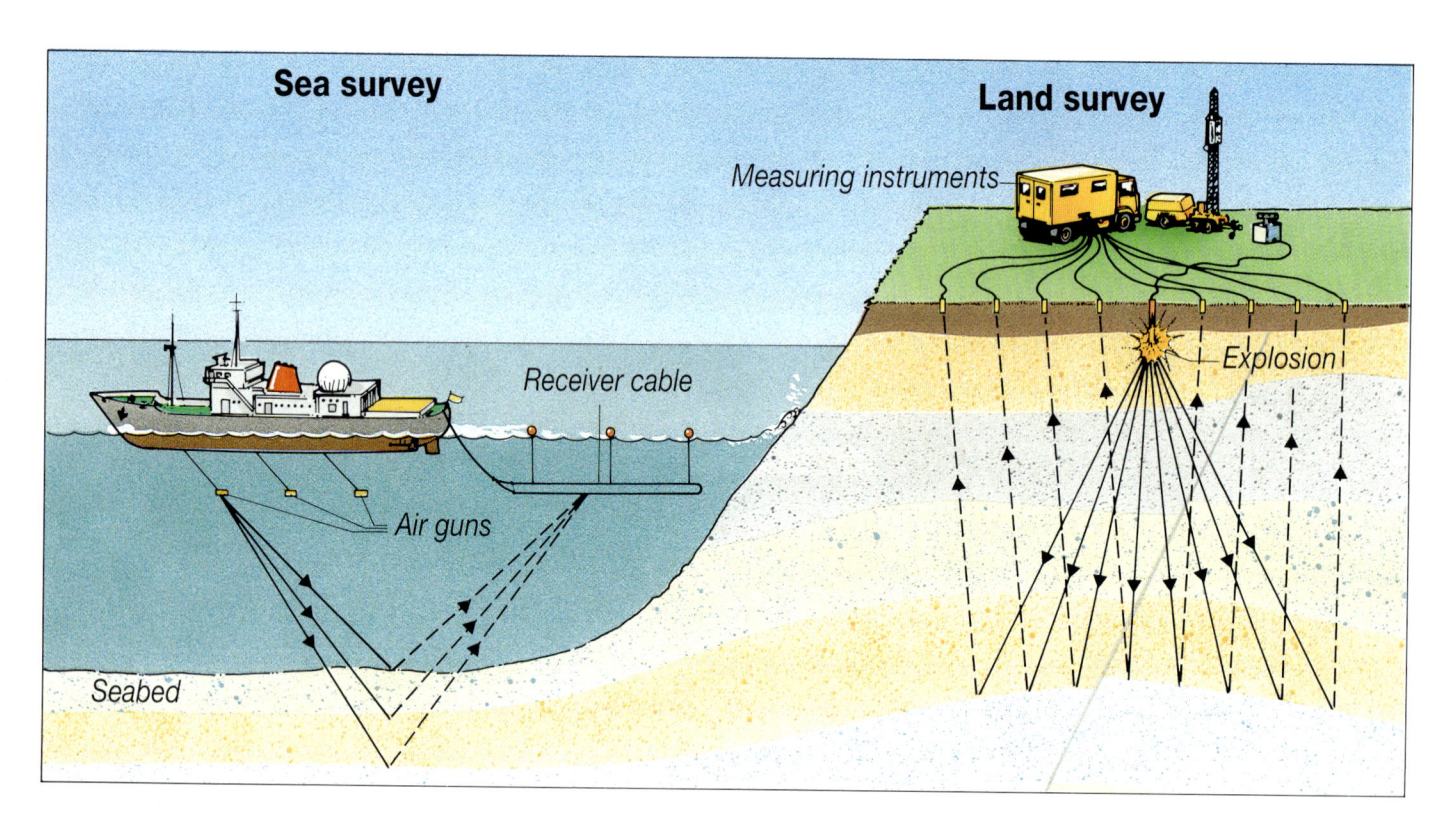

Geologists can undertake seismic surveys on land or at sea.

The deep-pit coal mine

The mine is a network of underground shafts and tunnels. In the shaft, elevators lift the miners up and down and take the coal out. Other shafts provide ventilation and cooling around the mine.

The coal is cut by the longwall method. A large machine, often a "shearer" or a "trepanner," goes along a tunnel, which can be over 650 feet long, scraping off large amounts of coal. A conveyer belt takes the coal away.

The miners' job is usually to make sure the machine is working correctly and to shift the props that hold up the roof. The miners must keep everything and everyone safe from explosions and rock falls. It is rare today, even in developing countries, for miners to swing a pick and shovel.

A coal-cutting shearer on a longwall coal-face.

Oil exploration in Australia. Australia imports a lot of oil and is eager to find more supplies of its own.

A uranium mining community in South Africa.

Explosions are set off and their effect on the rocks is measured by machines. Certain types of echoes show that there may be oil or gas in the ground. Once it is certain, the drilling can begin. Today, drilling is as likely to take place at sea as on land.

Uranium, the fuel for nuclear power, is a silvery metal that is very dense, or heavy. One thousand tons of ore is needed to produce every two tons of uranium. Uranium is mined in Canada, the United States, South Africa, Namibia, France, and Australia. Uranium mining is a very

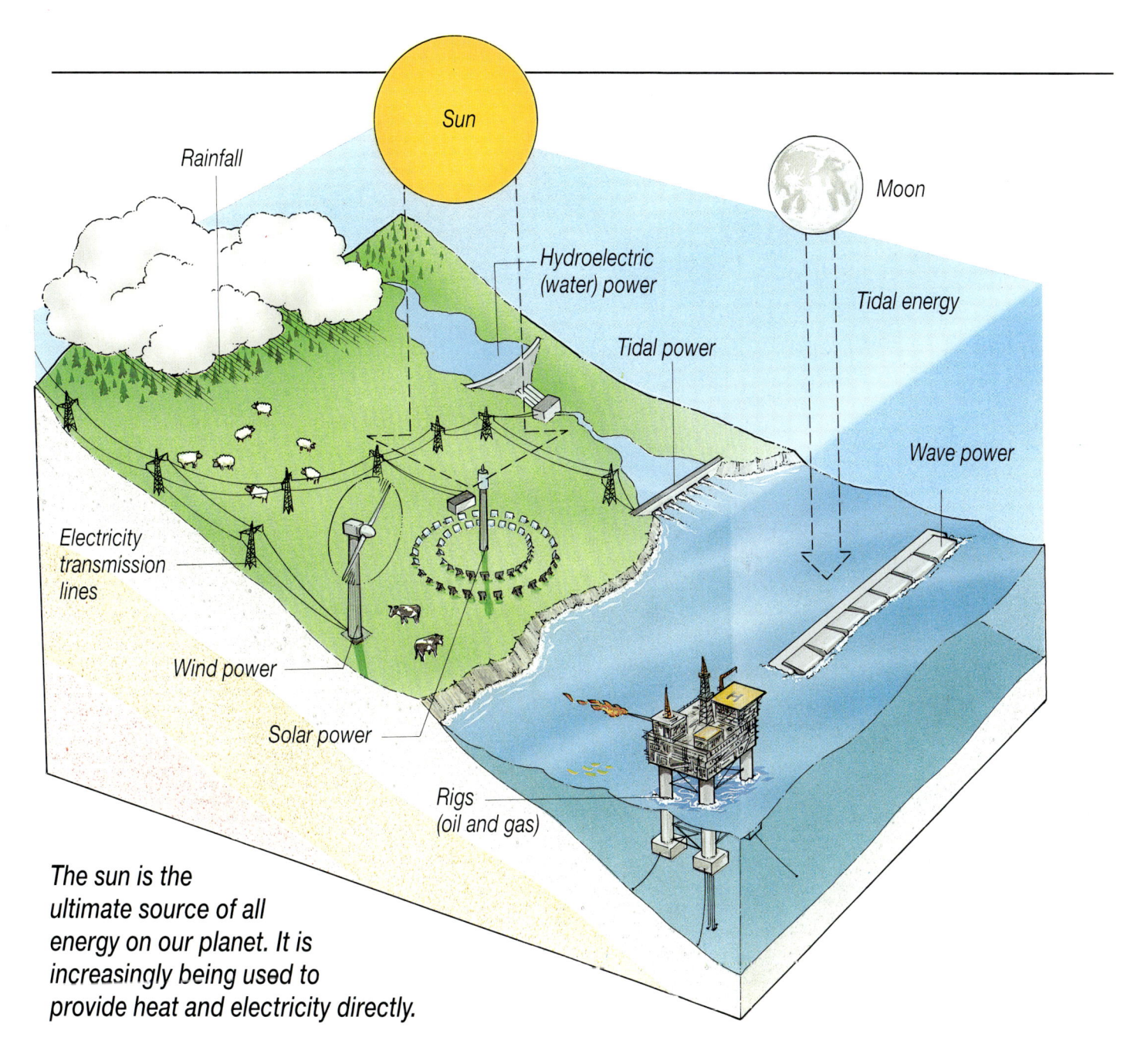

The sun is the ultimate source of all energy on our planet. It is increasingly being used to provide heat and electricity directly.

dangerous occupation because of the **radioactive** nature of the material.

The third resource for energy is alternative energy methods. All forms of energy originally came from the sun, but only recently could solar power be used directly.

Wind and water power are sometimes described as "second-hand solar power," because the sun's heat causes the movement of wind and water. We are now beginning to learn how best to extract energy from these renewable sources.

17

Creating power

Coal, gas, and sometimes oil are burned in power plants to produce electricity. The heat from the burning fuel boils water to make steam. The steam goes to the **turbine**, which turns very fast as the steam hits the blades, the way a windmill is turned by the wind. The spinning turbine drives the generator, which is a massive magnet spinning inside a coil of copper wire. This creates an electric current in the wire. The current is sent through the cables to the houses and businesses where it is needed.

In nuclear power plants the turbines are driven by steam in the same way, but the steam does

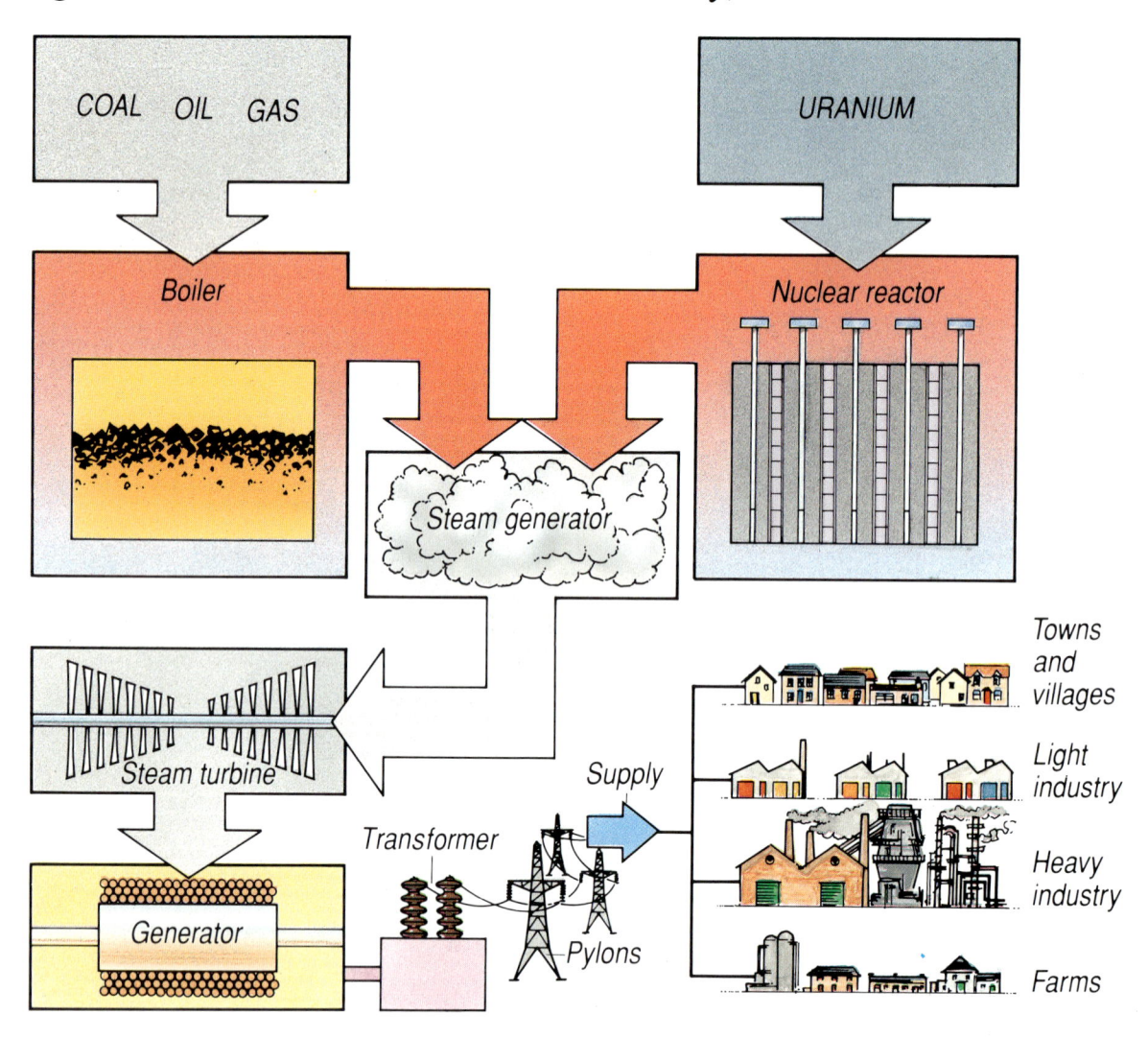

This diagram shows how fuels are used to generate electricity.

The control room monitors the workings of a nuclear power plant.

not come from burning fuel. Instead, uranium is used in what is called a nuclear reaction. The **atoms** of uranium in a reactor are made to split. Parts of atoms smash into other atoms, breaking them up and releasing a lot of heat. This heat is absorbed by a coolant fluid that becomes hot enough to produce the steam to drive the turbines.

Resources are also made into fuel used for transportation. Oil can be converted into gasoline for cars, diesel oil for trucks and buses, or kerosene (paraffin) for planes. The different kinds of engines work in different ways, but all drive a vehicle using the energy released when the fuel is burned or exploded.

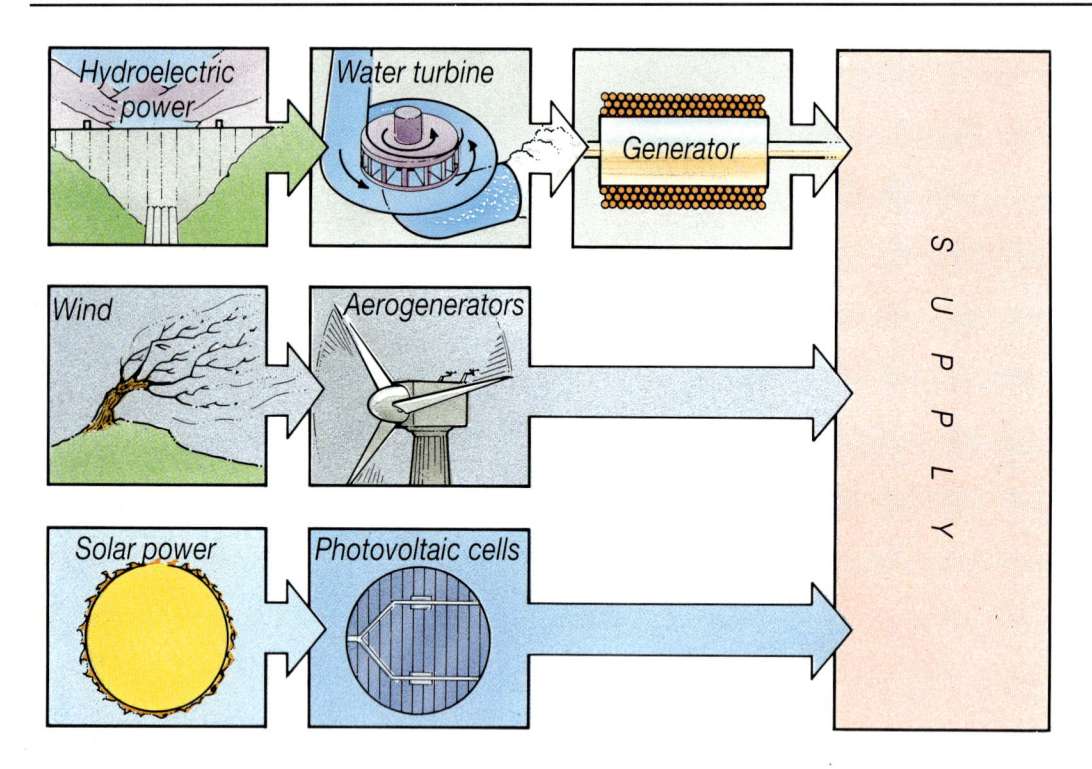

Left *This diagram shows how alternative sources of energy are used to produce power.*

Below *Hydroelectric plants in New Zealand, like this one, provide most of the country's electricity.*

Renewable forms of energy – solar, wind, and water power – are converted in many different ways. Superefficient solar panels are used around the world, and architects are designing buildings to make as much use of the sun's light and heat as possible. For years, solar electric cells, called photovoltaic cells, have been used to power calculators, but now they provide power for houses and whole towns in Australia and the United States.

Windmills called aerogenerators provide electricity. Wind farms with large numbers of turbines are common in the United States and are now being built in Europe.

Hydroelectric stations provide most of the electricity for Norway, New Zealand, and parts of Canada. In the future, wave power and tidal power may supply much of the world's electricity.

Combined Heat and Power (CHP) Plants

In a normal power plant that burns fossil fuels, about 70 percent of the energy from the fuel goes up the chimney in the form of steam and is wasted.

CHP plants make use of this waste heat. It flows in hot water piped into houses, offices, factories, and stores. It heats the buildings that are connected to the supply and the water that is used in the buildings.

This means that a CHP plant uses less energy overall, so the power plant gets more value out of its fuel. Another benefit is that the power plant makes less than half as much pollution for each unit of energy it produces.

Small CHP units are already used in factories in Britain, North America, and Australia. Some countries have large CHP units serving wide areas.

Above Wasteful steam rising from the cooling tower of a conventional power plant.

Below In a CHP system, heat, in the form of hot water, is supplied as well as electricity.

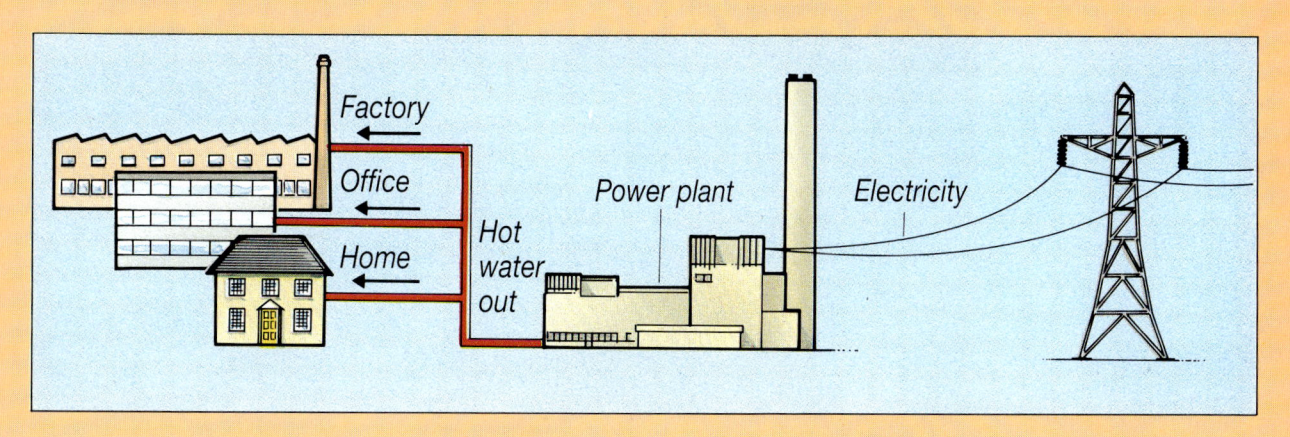

The environment

The main result of digging up raw materials is that, sooner or later, they will be gone. Certain metal ores, such as copper, lead, and tin, are now running low. In most parts of the world oil and gas will be used up quite soon.

The effects of mining on the environment are often easy to see. Strip mining leaves enormous holes, as if the landscape has been torn apart. All types of mining often leave large piles of waste material called spoil heaps. These can sometimes be shaped or planted with trees and grass, but it takes a long time for the land to return to its old state again.

More important is that the pollution from spoil heaps can contain dangerous material. The best known example of this is

Diamond mining in the nineteenth century at Kimberley Cape, South Africa, caused this blot on the landscape, called the "Big Hole."

The holding pond to collect acid drainage at an iron mine.

uranium mining, in which the spoil heaps contain radioactive material dug out of the ground. In other cases spoil heaps contain dangerous "heavy metals," like lead and mercury, or chemicals used to take the metal out of the ore.

All these materials pollute nearby rivers and lakes.

The consequences of clearing a forest are far-reaching. The soil becomes eroded so that nothing can grow. It washes away into the rivers, filling them with silt.

Acid rain

Acid rain is not always rain. The various acids come down to earth not just in rain, snow, and fog, but also in dry particles. The acids result from power plants, factories, and road vehicles. The main types of acid are sulfuric, from power plants and factories; and nitric, mainly from vehicles.

Acid rain attacks living plants, and many millions of trees have already been killed. It affects the soil, draining away nutrients that plants need. In rivers and lakes, fish and other creatures are killed by the metals, especially aluminum, that the acid causes to come out of the soil. In towns you can see the effects of acid rain on buildings and statues.

Above Acid rain speeded up the corrosion of this stone statue.

Below The cycle of acid rain causes serious environmental problems.

With no soil, there is nothing to hold back the water after heavy rains, as the soil of the forest floor and the trees would have done. This causes heavy flooding, which does more damage and endangers people. Today Bangladesh suffers worse floods than in times past because of loss of forests in the foothills of the Himalayas.

Smelting and manufacturing from metals produce air pollution. Chemicals causing acid rain, like sulfur dioxide, come from non-iron smelting, which also sends out heavy metals and poisons like arsenic into the air.

Burning fossil fuels causes two major problems, acid rain and global warming. Global warming, from the "greenhouse effect," is the warming of Earth's **atmosphere** caused by the buildup of gases that trap some of the sun's heat instead of letting it escape into space. The main greenhouse gas is carbon dioxide, which comes from burning fossil fuels. Scientists are not sure exactly what the effects will be, but there will almost certainly be some rise in sea levels and climate changes in some parts of the world. This means we must burn fossil fuels as little as possible.

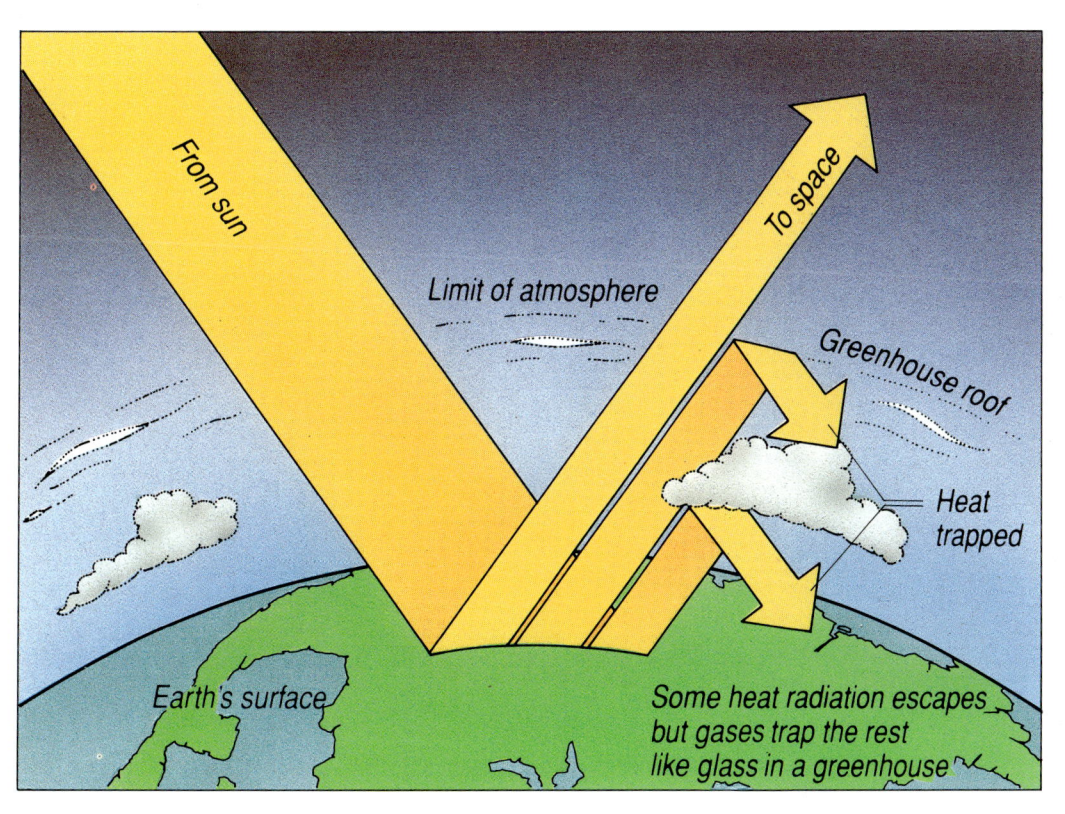

The earth would be too cold if there were no "greenhouse effect." Problems are caused when the atmosphere overheats because of the buildup of extra greenhouse gases.

Water

Water is always flowing, except when it is frozen as thick ice sheets. Water moves through what is called the water cycle. In the cycle it rises from the ground, the lakes, and the seas into the air, where it forms clouds. Then it falls back to Earth, where it flows along the rivers to lakes and seas or goes underground. It rises because of evaporation from lakes and seas and **transpiration** from plants.

Each adult needs over five quarts of water per day. We take water into our bodies by drinking, eating, and breathing. We lose it by urination, sweating, and breathing out water vapor. Most of the world's water is used for farming and industry. As countries become more developed, they use more water. By the year 2000, it is thought that the world will use ten times more water than it did in 1900.

All plants need water to survive. These crops are growing in a dry area, so they are watered by an irrigation system.

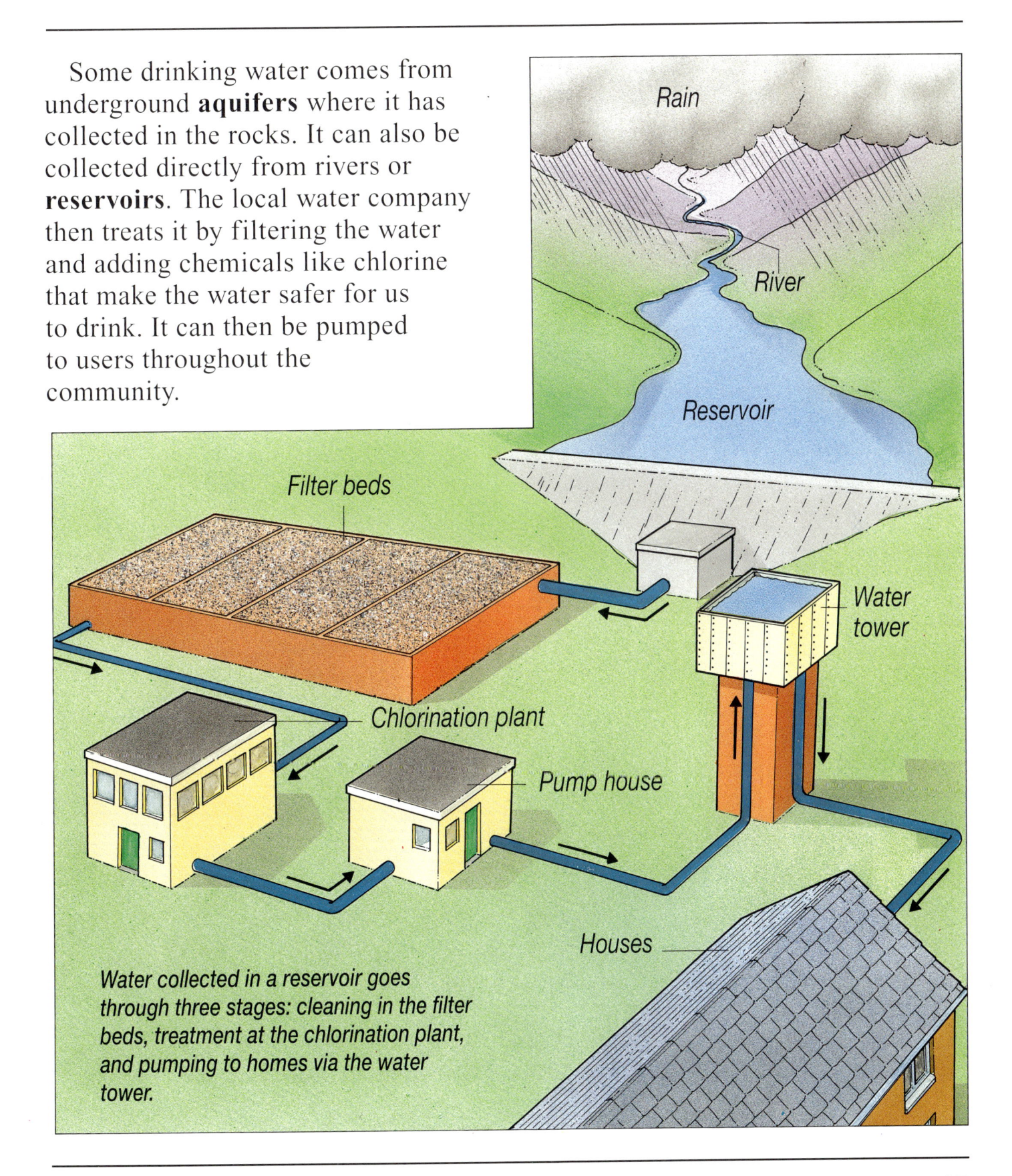

Some drinking water comes from underground **aquifers** where it has collected in the rocks. It can also be collected directly from rivers or **reservoirs**. The local water company then treats it by filtering the water and adding chemicals like chlorine that make the water safer for us to drink. It can then be pumped to users throughout the community.

Water collected in a reservoir goes through three stages: cleaning in the filter beds, treatment at the chlorination plant, and pumping to homes via the water tower.

Recycling

Much of what we throw away could be used again. Recycling puts "garbage" to good use. Recycling helps preserve precious resources because it saves on the use of raw materials and energy. It also reduces the pollution caused when the waste is dumped.

Glass can be remelted. This is better than making fresh glass from raw materials, but it is even better to reuse the bottle whole. Metals can be recycled by being resmelted and then used to make other new items. The metals to recycle from an ordinary household are aluminum and steel from cans. Scrap from cars gives several different metals for recycling.

Paper is easy to recycle. Every home and office should have a paper recycling routine. Plastics are the worst problem because they do not **biodegrade** (break down) easily. They are also hard to recycle and cause harmful pollution when burned. It is important to use as few plastics as possible, and then only ones that are recyclable or biodegradable.

Cans and bottles are some of the household items that can be recycled.

Recycling in Seattle, Washington

Seattle, Washington, is a world leader in recycling. In 1985 it became very expensive for the city to dispose of garbage by the usual means, so many people began to think of alternatives.

Today, each household, school, and place of work has separate containers for different types of trash. There are containers in many parts of the city for large items, such as old washing machines, to be recycled.

The people of Seattle now recycle about a third of their waste, and aim to recycle nearly two-thirds by 1998. This will include not only the usual items like glass, paper, plastics, and aluminum, but also waste that causes special pollution problems, such as oil and batteries.

Most important, they are researching and planning so that, by the year 2010, not just recycling, but creating less waste in the first place, will become a way of life.

Although bottle banks have appeared in many towns, it is much better to reuse bottles.

Glossary

Aquifer Rocks under the ground that store water in the tiny spaces between them.
Atmosphere The envelope of air around the earth.
Atom The smallest part of an element.
Biodegrade To break down into separate parts when buried in the ground.
Blast furnace A tall tower lined with bricks that heats the materials in it by blasting them with hot air.
Bucket-wheel excavator An enormous moving digger that scoops out coal or ore with buckets attached to the edge of a wheel.
Ceramic Made from clay or sand.
Efficient Making the best use of materials or energy, and wasting as little as possible.
Element A single chemical substance, not mixed with any other substance.
Erode To blow or wash away soil.
Fertilize To put substances into the soil to make plants grow better.
Fossil fuel A fuel such as oil, gas, or coal that was formed millions of years ago from the bodies of dead plants and animals.
Impurities Unwanted matter, such as dirt and rocks.
Magnetic sensor A machine that detects magnetic fields in the earth.
Manufacturing Making products in factories.
Mechanized Using machinery to do work.
Minerals Materials that are found in rocks in the ground.
Molten The condition of a metal when it is very hot and melted into liquid form.
Ores Rocks containing metals.
Pollution Damage to the environment caused by waste materials.
Pulp A mass of broken-down wood fibers and liquid.
Radar Radio waves sent out so that the pattern of their echo can be read when they come back.
Radioactive Giving off particles of atoms, called electrons and neutrons, as is done by certain minerals like uranium.
Refining Separating different materials, using heat, other chemicals, or electricity.
Renewable Able to be restored and used again.
Reservoir A lake formed behind a dam to supply people with water.
Resources All the materials from which we can obtain what we need to survive.
Silica sand The main ingredient of glass that is found naturally in sand as a material called quartz.
Smelting Heating ores to get the metal out.
Transpiration Plants giving out water through their stems and leaves.
Turbine A device powered by steam or water pressure that can drive a generator.
Ventilation The means of providing a supply of fresh air to a place.
Walking draglines Large diggers attached to long chains. They are moved along like a crane, tearing out large amounts of coal or ore.

Books to read

Dineen, Jacqueline. *Wood and Paper*. Hillside, NJ: Enslow Publishers, 1987.

Jackman, Wayne. *Gas*. Resources. New York: Thomson Learning, 1993.

Jennings, Terry. *Water*. Chicago: Childrens Press, 1989.

Kalman, Bobbie. *Natural Resources*. New York: Crabtree Publishing, 1987.

Peckham, Alex. *Resources Control*. New York: Franklin Watts, 1990.

Rickard, Graham. *Oil*. Resources. New York: Thomson Learning, 1993.

Notes for activities

Ask your teacher if you can visit a paper mill, steelworks, glass factory, or brickyard to find out how their products are made. Ask questions about how materials are recycled and how the factory gets rid of waste.

Investigate the types of energy being used locally – on your street, in your neighborhood, and in your town. Also investigate energy saving: You could ask people whether they have insulation in their roof, walls, or floor, and if so, how much.

Find out how efficiently people use energy in their home or place of business. Find out how much money is spent on energy each year. Then find out the volume of the building (by multiplying height by length by width in feet). Divide the money by the total cubic feet. Compare and discuss your results.

Carry out pollution experiments near your home. These include checking water samples from different parts of a river, investigating the effects of acid rain or other air pollution, and using growing plants to find out ozone levels. Write to organizations in your area that can help you set up these experiments.

Investigate the possibility of a school-based recycling operation. You could encourage your friends to recycle unwanted bottles, cans, and paper by storing them on the school site. Make sure that you have the materials collected regularly.

Index

acid rain 24, 25
aerogenerators 20
aquifers 27
atmosphere 25
Australia 6, 14, 15, 20, 21

biodegrading 28
Britain 14, 20, 21

Canada 16, 20
ceramics 12
chemicals 13, 23
Combined Heat and
    Power (CHP) 21

drilling 14, 16

effects on environment 5,
    13, 22-25
    global warming 25
    greenhouse effect 25
electricity 18
erosion 9, 23
Europe 14, 20

fertilizers 8
floods 25
forestry 8, 23, 25
fossil fuels 14-15, 18-19,
    21, 25

glass 12, 29

hydroelectricity 20

impurities 10
industry 5, 24

magnetic sensors 14
metals 5, 6-7, 10-11, 23,
    24, 28, 29
Middle East, the 14
minerals 6, 14
mining 6-7, 15, 16

New Zealand 20
North Sea, the 14
Norway 20
nuclear
    power 14, 18-19
    reaction 19

ores 5, 6, 10-11

paper 13, 28, 29
plastics 28, 29
pollution 5, 13, 21, 22-25,
    28
power plants 19, 21, 24

radar 14
radioactivity 17, 23

rain forests 8
recycling 5, 28-29
refining 11
renewable resources 8,
    17, 20
reservoirs 27

satellites 14
silica sand 12
solar power 17, 20
soil heaps 22

timber 4, 5, 8, 13
turbines 18, 19

uranium 14, 16, 17, 19, 23

vehicles 19, 24

water 4-5, 26-27
    cycle 26
    power 17, 20
wind farms 20
wind power 17, 20

Picture acknowledgments

The publishers would like to thank the following for allowing their pictures to be used in this book: AEA Technology 16; British Coal *title page*, 15 top; Bruce Coleman Ltd. 22 (Gerald Cubitt), 24 (Adrian Davies), 29 (C. James); J. Allan Cash Ltd. 4, 6, 15 (bottom); Pilkington Glass PLC 12; Tony Stone Worldwide *front cover* (Simon Jauncey), *back cover* (David Woodfall), 5 (Lester Lefkowitz), 7 (Dave Saunders), 8 (Glen Allison), 10 (Keith Wood), 11 (Charles Thatcher), 13 top, 19 (Jon Riley), 21 (Frank Cezus), 23 (Thomas Braise), 26 (D. C. Lowe), 28 (Dennis O'Clair); Tropix 9; Wayland Picture Library 13 (Angus Blackburn), 20 (New Zealand High Commission). Artwork is by Nick Hawken.